> *"I say the world is lovely and that loveliness is enough."*
> *~ Robert William Buchanan*

Memories don't have to sit on a shelf or be stuffed in a drawer. Make a small shrine with a postcard, shell and a bit of sand, just enough to bring back a special moment.

Memory Shrine

MATERIALS:
Design Originals Collage Paper #0589 At the Beach • *Silver Crow* Shrine • *ARTchix Studio* Fabric Art Woman • Vial • Sand • Starfish • *JewelCraft* Crystal rhinestone • Wooden skewer • The Ultimate! glue

INSTRUCTIONS:
Inside Box: Trace the back of the container onto Beach paper and cut out. Glue into shrine with The Ultimate!. • Spread a thin layer of glue on the printed side of the lady and press it to the inside of the window. • Glue the starfish behind the lady on the background paper. • Fill a small vial with sand and glue it to the bottom of the shrine.

Outside Box: Dip the tip of a skewer in glue. Put a dot of glue where you want the rhinestone to set. Dip the skewer in the glue again and use it to pick up the rhinestone. Glue rhinestone in place. • Glue seashells around the top of the shrine.

1. Pick up a dot of glue with a skewer and place on project.

2. Dip skewer back into the glue. Pick up a rhinestone.

3. Set rhinestone in place.

Poem In A Can

"Poetry is a way of taking life by the throat!"
~ Robert Frost

MATERIALS:
Design Originals (Mounts #0988 Small White, Transparency Sheet #0560 Objects) • 8mm Film canister • 10 *Tara/Fredrix* canvas coasters • *Foofala* Fiber Tails Fragments twill tape • Two poems that can be divided into 5 segments • *Jacquard* (Black Neopaque paint, Bronze Lumiere) • *Mayco* Dark Bronze Magic Metallic paint • Gloss Medium • Gel Medium Regular Matte • *Krylon* Copper Leafing pen • *Time to Stamp* Autumn fibers • *ARTchix Studio* Fabric Art • *Papers by Catherine* Grafiche Tassotti-Butterfly • Old dictionary page • Assorted collage images of women • Beads • Small tags • Elastic Thread • Craft knife • Awl • Hammer • Fine grit sandpaper for metal • Sponge • The Ultimate! glue

1. Space coasters evenly. Glue ribbons to coasters.

Poems and quotes are great ways to spark an emotion or thought in our art. Here two poems are illustrated, one on each side of the coaster accordion. You could use your own prose, or use your favorite quotes. If you want to go purely decorative, try using this technique for a travel journal.

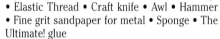

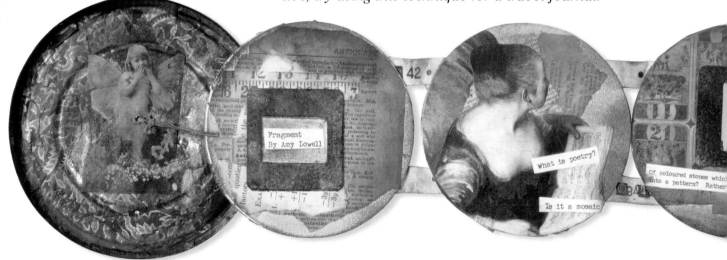

INSTRUCTIONS:

Prep: Choose the poems, quotes or themes for this project. Divide the words into five panels or if you use both sides for one idea, ten panels total. Gather collage material that relates to your theme.

Construction: Lay out 5 coasters. Lay the twill or ribbon between the five coasters. Arrange the tape and the coasters so they are evenly spaced and lay evenly on the coasters. • Remove the twill from the first coaster. Apply a liberal amount of gel medium to the bottom coaster. Position the twill on top of the gel. Repeat on the remaining coasters. Make sure the coasters are spaced so they will accordion fold. • Apply a liberal amount of gel medium to the bottom coaster. Press gently to the bottom coaster over the twill. Let dry.

Collage: Decide where you want your windows. Trace the mount onto the coaster. • Use a craft knife to carefully cut your holes. Carefully cut just outside the lines. • Collage, ink, paint and stamp over the coasters and mounts as desired. • Glue the transparency over the window and then glue the mount over the transparency.

Poem: Print out your words. Cut them into segments and glue to coasters.

Can: Use an awl and punch two holes in the middle of both film canisters. Use gloss medium as an adhesive and collage the inside of each canister. Let dry. • Lightly sand the outside of the canister. • Paint the outside of the canister with Black. Let dry. • Paint a second coat with Dark Bronze paint. Let dry. • Glue Fabric Art Image over holes on top of canister. Let dry. • Use an awl to punch holes through the fabric art. • Sponge Bronze paint over image and can. Let dry.

Fibers: Cut a thick bunch of fibers 12" long. From the outside, thread the fibers through the holes, making a loop on the inside. Pull the threads through so you have 2 even strands on the outside of the can. Thread Black elastic cord through the hole in the first coaster and the loop of fibers. Make sure the elastic stretches enough for the coasters to fit in the canister. Tie the ends. • Turn to the outside of the lid. Wrap fibers with another ribbon or cord. • String beads, tags, and charms on fibers as desired. • Thread another Black elastic cord through the holes in the bottom canister from the inside. Even up the ends. Thread one end through the last coaster. Make sure the elastic stretches enough for the coasters to fit in canister. Tie the ends.

> *"There are only two ways to live your life. One is as though nothing is a miracle. The other is as though everything is a miracle."*

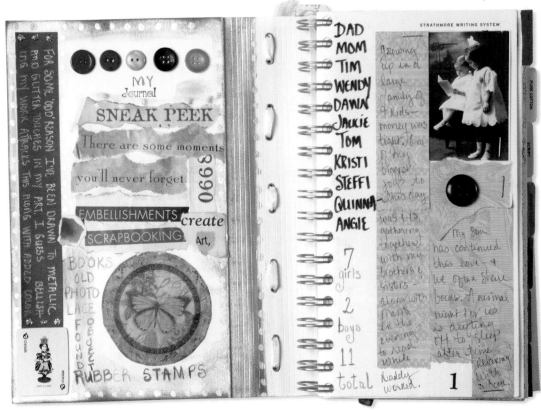

Growing up in a large family of nine children, one of my biggest joys to this day was and is gathering together with my brothers and sisters along with Mama in the evenings to read while Daddy worked.

My son has continued this love of reading and we often share books. We still enjoy drifting off to sleep after relaxing with a book.

Make the first page of your book uniquely yours. On my first page, I used collage to explain my approach to this book. It was fun tearing out words from magazines and writing with pencils and metallic pens.

This page holds two examples of journaling. A happy memo is colored in to give it emphasis. The daily notes are handwritten in ink.

Use your page to play with interesting textures and unusual materials. I decorated a bottle cap with an eye and placed it beside a quote about "vision".

Old objects decorate the upper portion of the page - a worn button, a rusty heart, a remnant from an old book. Arranging objects that would not normally be found together make the art interesting. This simple collage conveys a secret meaning - I still love old books. If your art has a message you want to share, express it with a journal entry.

If you don't feel like making your own journal, here's a great idea: alter a paper sample book into a fun and easy journal.

You can find a paper sample book at your local paper supply store or ask a printer for an outdated copy.

Paper Sample Journal

by Jackie Hull

MATERIALS:
Paper Sample book • Assorted rubber stamps (Numbers, Women) • *Clearsnap* (Rollagraph, Assorted wheels, Ancient Page inks: Sienna, Mango, Black) • Ribbons • Eyelets • Buttons • Beads • Cardstock • Magazine pictures and words • Tags • Eyelet tools • *USArtQuest* PPA

INSTRUCTIONS:
Spine: Set 10 eyelets in the spine of the book. Thread ribbons through eyelets. Tie ribbon ends in knots along the outside of the spine. Decorate tags with stamps and buttons as desired. Hang tags from ribbons.

Cover: Stamp image for front of book. Cut a cardstock mat slightly larger and glue the image to the mat with PPA. • Collage the cover with stamps and papers as desired.

Inside: Rollagraph the edges of the papers. Stamp page numbers. Collage magazine words and images to pages. Decorate with beads, buttons, wire, fibers, etc. as desired. • Record your journal entries.

...continued on pages 8 - 9

"Beauty of style and harmony and grace and good rhythm depend upon simplicity."

~ Plato

1. Edge the pages with a rollagraph.

2. Stamp numbers on each page.

continued from pages 6 - 7...

Need a place to put neat ideas? Why not give them a journal page? This page holds a magazine photo of a garter belt clip holding an old French print.

Practice the art of collage by grouping images and text that express a common theme.

Your art book is already full of color and texture. It is a joy to view and touch. Now, add smell to the senses being tantalized by your work. The vellum envelope contains fragrant lavender seeds.

Go to your studio and make ART! Nurture the things that feed your creative spirit. Practice and learn to execute your work extremely well. Rejuvenate your soul by visiting inspiring places and people. Most importantly, don't let housework interfere with your Art work.

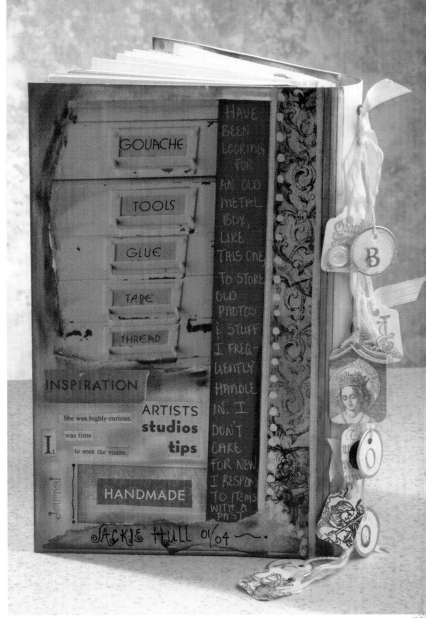

> *"A bird does not fear falling for it has never fallen before. So we must act as the bird and block out our fears. Then we will be able to soar higher than we ever imagined."*
>
> ~ Kevin Wassie

This is the back cover of the book. The tiny collaged words say "She was highly curious. It was time to seek the vision." This statement really sums up the spirit conveyed by this wonderful book of art.

Notice how the pages are not all the same size. Even before you use them, having stacked pages give the book an added layer of dimension. You can choose which page is the size for your memo or art that day. Remember, no one said you have to use the pages in order.

Is there a particular image or color combination that pleases you? Put it in your book and record your thoughts about it. Your art becomes "personal" when you allow the viewer to know what you were thinking.

Store your secrets in this decorative envelope. Since it is glued to the page, your secrets won't get lost.

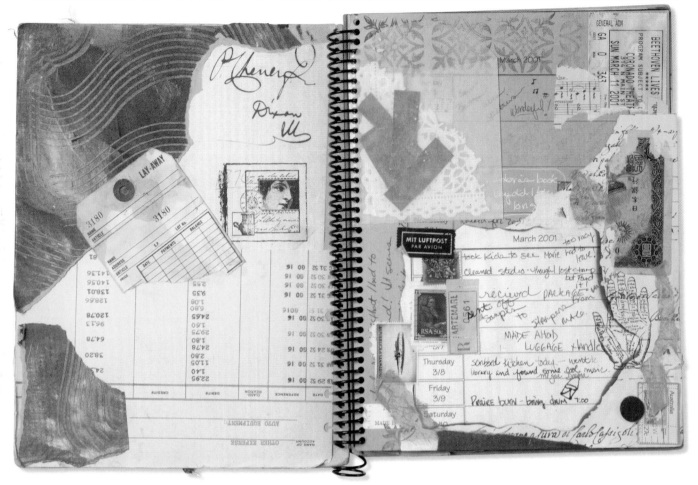

Does the old-fashioned idea of a journal bother you? Would you like to keep some kind of journal, but facing all those blank pages turns you off? I made this project the first year I was in an altered calendar round robin. I couldn't find the exact kind of journal or calendar I wanted, so I put everything I ever wanted into one big journal and I came up with this monster. A lot of it is personal preference.

Think about how you want to use this. Will it be a journal? If so, can you fill one page per week? Or does it make more sense to make a week a half a page? Or a month a page? Do you want the days numbered for a specific year? Or does the idea of a "Book of Days" that can be applied to any year sound less stressful?

Will it be a round robin? If so, use sturdy items and book board for the cover so it survives all the handling. Will it be mailed? Think about size for mailing. Choose a size that fits easily in a priority envelope.

Don't forget to be inventive. Start on any day in the year. Who says your calendar has to start on January 1? Start on your birthday and have the first thing be a birthday card to yourself. Use pages ripped out of old musty books, old maps, junk mail, envelopes and tags. This is meant to be a visual journal of the evidence of one year of your life, or one month of the lives of 11 of your friends and you. Enjoy!

> "Reach high, for stars lie hidden in your soul. Dream deep, for every dream precedes the goal."
> ~ Ralph Vaull

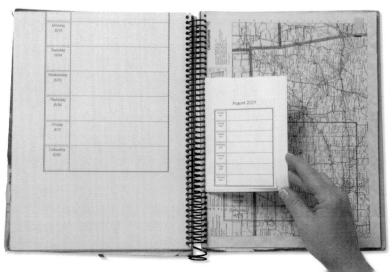

Altered Calendar Books

MATERIALS:
Coil Binder • Papers • *Zettiology* journaling stamps • Ink pads • Envelopes • Vellum envelopes • Tags • 2 pieces of matboard • Optional: Printed calendar for desired year • Repositionable double-stick tape • *USArtQuest* PPA

INSTRUCTIONS:
Cover: If the covers are not sturdy, adhere a sheet of matboard to each one with PPA. Collage, stamp, or paint the covers as desired.

Plan: If desired, print grid calendar pages using your home computer. Cut them out. • If you are going to make a blank journal, decide how many pages you want to include.

Prep: Gather cardstocks, vellums, book pages, paper bags, envelopes in all sizes and kinds of materials, tags, book pages, maps, printed collage papers, patterned papers, junk mail, and anything else you might want to include in your calendar. Remember there are 52 weeks to a year, so you want at least 26 pages. • If any of the papers are one-sided, glue another piece of paper to the back to make it two sided.

Organize: Lay the paper out in the order you like. I use a big kitchen table and lay them side by side, then travel across to the sofa etc. Get the big picture here. If you are using calendar pages, glue the calendar grids to the pages, envelopes, etc. • Once you have the paper in order, add your envelopes, tags and other cool stuff that will be bound together.

Binding: Use removable double-sided tape to attach the small envelopes to the large pages. Be sure to have the left side line up. This is where the coil binding will be and this will hold the pages and the envelopes together. If they are not bound together, the tags will fall out. • If you have a coil binding machine, do it yourself or go to an office supply and copy store. It is very inexpensive to do.

Finish:
Remove the double-sided tape. Stamp with your journal stamps and have fun!

...continued on pages 12 - 13

continued from pages 10 - 11...

If you enjoyed keeping a diary when you were younger, you may rekindle that interest with a page designed to note the tiny miracles that occur every day. When you get up in the morning and are thrilled with the bunny in your back yard, or see that first swallowtail butterfly, record it on a page like this one.

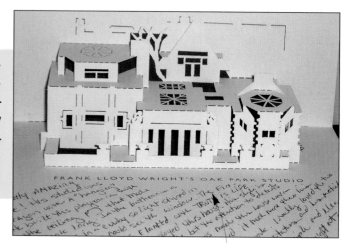

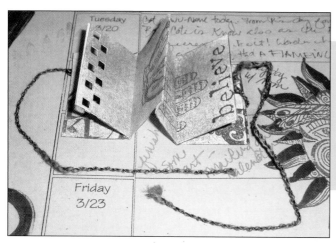

Use your calendar journal to store the cards and letters you receive from loved ones. Now you will have a safe place to keep that very special valentine, or the card that came with the flowers on your anniversary.

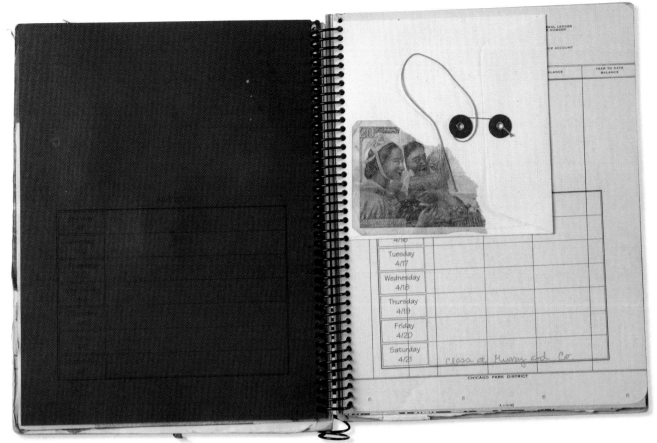

Here's a great way to use those odd size and left over envelopes. Attach them right into the binding, so you don't have to tape them to a page. The envelopes will turn freely, giving you a place to put tiny treasures, love notes, or wonderful ideas you have.

Decorate an envelope with "dreams" and put all your wishes inside.

This calendar grid is ready for your journal entries.

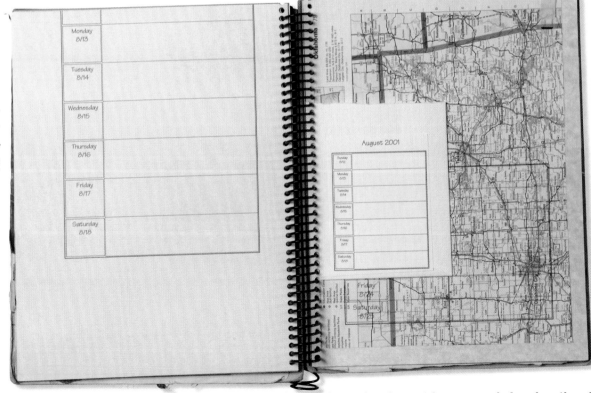

Are you going on vacation in August? Use the calendar grid to record the details of your trip. Use the back of the grid to list the "don't forget to pack" items. And, since getting there is half the fun, don't forget to include the map! You can make a pocket on the back of this page to hold all the brochures. Use a vellum envelope to store entry tickets and other memorabilia.

1. Cut foamcore into a shape.

2. Adhere paper to foamcore with gel medium.

3. Use a palette knife to slap on modeling paste.

You can alter foamcore and turn it into little collages in frames with a bit of wire and some light modeling paste.

These easy and inexpensive framed art pieces are easy and a lot of fun.

Foam Board Frames

by Ellen Gradman

MATERIALS:
Foamcore • *Golden* Light Modeling Paste • *Jacquard* Gold Lumiere paint • Acrylic paints • *Artistic Wire* • Collage materials • Beads • Fibers • Palette knife • Gel medium

INSTRUCTIONS:
Foamcore: Cut a piece of foamcore into a shape.
Collage: Adhere decorative papers with gel medium. Let dry. • Stamp collage if desired. • Add paint or glaze as desired to blend the edges of the collage.
Frame: Use your palette knife to slap on light modeling paste. Build the edges of the foamcore into a framed shape. This needs to be done in a slap-dash fashion for a rugged feel. Let dry. Add another layer if needed. • Paint with Gold. Let dry.
Finish: Insert wire into the edges of the frame to create a hanger. Add beads. Twist ends into spirals and shapes for a decorative effect.

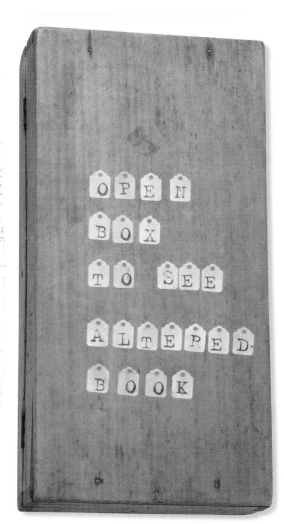

Altered Book
with Wooden Box

by Virginia Simpson-Magruder

MATERIALS:
Old wooden box • *Nostalgiques* Tag stickers • Book that fits in the box • Assorted stamps • Ink pads • Collage materials • Beaded ribbon • Fibers • Ephemera • UHU glue stick

INSTRUCTIONS:
Box: Add title stickers to the front of the box. • Collage and decorate the inside of the box as desired.

      This old wooden box protects and houses my first altered book. I had joined the Yahoo Altered Book group. I purchased and read Beth's book, Altered Books 101, and went out immediately to purchase a book I could use as a technique book. I found it in a secondhand bookstore. This old pronunciation book is filled with archaic words, with a few definitions thrown in. Even though the pages were thin, they were of a lovely quality and fairly sturdy, allowing me to experiment with different materials. I also loved the feel of the book. It is small and comfortably fits in my hand.

      With respect to altering, I've left the cover alone, except for some iridescent Golden acrylics and some stenciling. However, the book evolved from being a technique book to something with a life of its own. It became organic and quite beautiful. It also became a goodwill emissary for altered books! I wanted to show it to a friend, so I plopped it into an old artist's box for protection. My friend said that I should keep it in the box and write something that tells people what an altered book is, so they know what it is they are looking at. So, I created a tag for the left hand side of the box that describes what an altered book is. I printed the words out on an ink jet transparency and attached it with rivets to the tag. The tag and the box seem to encourage people to interact with the book. They can hold the box on their lap and not feel like they are going to "damage a piece of art." The tag encourages them to pick up the book and turn the pages. People tend to spend more time interacting with this book than any others I have, and I think that's because of the way it's presented.

...continued on pages 18 - 19

The Empress

I wanted a dramatic interactive first spread. This simple design engages the viewer immediately. I began with a photo of a Saudi door, handhewn and built centuries ago. I applied Lumiere Violet Gold to this page and stamped with a Penny Black design. I placed Memories letters on the door that read "Enter". I tore the preceding page (down and across and then up and across) to create a swinging "arm". I glued a tarot card to the back of the swinging arm. I sponged some Violet Gold Lumiere on the edges of the card. The paint/stamp technique was repeated on the preceding page. To my mind, the Empress serves as a "guard" to the door, swinging back and forth, either preventing or allowing access to the rest of the book. "The Empress" card comes from the Tarot Maddonni deck Ets. J.M. Simon, France Cartes.

Raptor: If I Had Wings

I usually start a spread with one image that I feel pulled to. In this case it was the brown Harris hawk. The feeling of freedom and beauty of its outstretched wings commanded me to place it on the page. Then what? I often play with perspective. I had a picture of a medieval city, so I tore its edges on a slant, colored them lightly with Cat's Eye pad, then glued it on the left-hand page. I used Lumiere again as my backdrop. To create some dimension under the bird I created "bars" from a beautiful two-toned green/copper ribbon. I mounted the bird using foam squares so it seems to fly above the page.

Alchemist's Wanderings

The basic elements for this spread came from a color deck swap where I chose gold. We were asked to write about our associations with the color, and alchemy and transformation came to mind. Hence, I created a collage showing a medieval alchemist with a goblet, a gold sun, and gold coins or pentacles spilling about. I backed the card with a bumpy, handmade gold paper using the Xyron. I had to trim the edges and I had tons of this stuff, so I challenged myself to create a spread using the sticky gold trimmings! So I created a web or "forest," which traps the alchemist on his journey, as well as a few of his "treasures" including the large gold charms that I happened to have in my supplies.

Church of the Blood

I loved this magazine image because of its perspective. It's perfect for drawing you into the spread. I used Lumiere Metallic Bronze for the background, and then I floated a couple over the "water." This image by itself is almost too strong so I printed it out as a transparency. This is a good technique to do when you want images to be more suggestive or evocative and to blend in with the whole spread.

continued from pages 16 - 17...

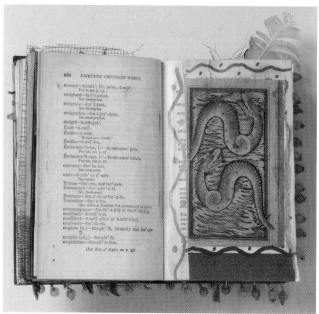

▲ If you have an image that appeals to you or stirs your imagination, dedicate a page to it in your altered book. This one was decorated with Lumiere after it was glued down.

◄ Wings of Desire

This is a very bold page! I think it is the first page I ever painted using Lumiere paint. I love Lumiere. The paint glides onto a surface so easily and adds pizzazz because it is iridescent, almost luminous. In this spread, I first picked out the word "desire" on the page. Then I stamped the word "Desire" along with an image of a woman from Frantic Stamper. I had a square of woven paper and created a pocket using eyelets. Underneath I placed a valentine heart I found in London, and then placed three silk plant leaves coming out of the pocket. The images of the plants were from a magazine article. They were such a great red and green pattern, and had a sultry, almost carnivorous feel. I had to include them in the spread. I sponged the gutter with Cat's Eye ink.

▲ Eve - A Homage to Grant Wood

This spread was one of the first I created in this book. I just loved this postcard of an early Grant Wood painting, "Eve" that I bought at a London museum. It's so primitive and the colors he uses were particularly appealing to me. The alphabet stamps are from Stampers Anonymous. Cat's Eyes were dragged across the page for color background.

◄ This is my "Wish You Were Here" page. Every time I see this image, taken from a magazine, I wish I was there. The opposite page is decorated with my representation of a garden gate.

▲ A Medieval Theatre: The Marriage of Sadie & Figaro

In this spread I used images left over from a techniques swap. My technique was 3-D images. I printed the stones from a Dover clip art book and created 3-D rosettes from them. Then I used a couple more images, the boar and the wolf's head, and began constructing a theatre, making puppets out of them using coffee stirrers and creating pockets from the rosettes to hold the puppets. That reminded me of Punch and Judy, hence the title of "A Medieval Theatre".

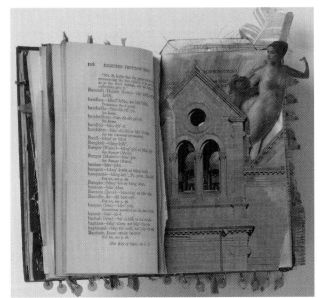

Ascension

I like using buildings and architecture in my altered art because they give the pages a strong feeling of solidity. They make a statement and people have strong associations with the images of houses and churches. This magazine image of a church in Santa Fe, although beautiful, presented the problem of being too heavy so I added the image of Cupid and Psyche and gave them the ability to soar above the church. They are mounted on a thin mounting board and then on a coffee stirrer. I created a pocket in the back of the church, which the pair can slide in and out of. I used Cat's Eyes and oil pastels on the background.

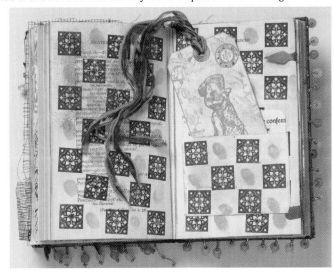

Medieval Courtship

I had created this tag and wanted to find a home for it, so I decided to create an altered book spread. Using a technique shown in Beth's Altered Books 101, I stamped a square in a checkerboard pattern. I added glitter to the center of each stamped image. I repeated the pattern on a library pocket and glued it to the page to create a home for the tag!

Athena's Hallway

This image is from a book on Greece. It seemed very shrine-like, so I glued about 15 pages together, then glued the image down. I cut out the center doorway and down through the glued pages behind to create a tiny niche. The owl is a sticker. The day after I created this page, I went out to the barn and there was a barn owl's feather in the aisle. It was the perfect complement for the book and I laid it down over the page, which I painted with Lumiere paint. I love it when things just magically appear!

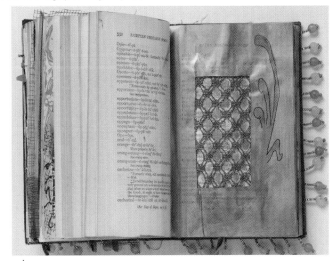

Confession

This is an unfinished page. I cut out a square from two sets of pages that I had glued together and then glued a piece of gold fabric mesh in between the two sets. I used Lumiere Sun Gold and stenciled the leaf and scallop motif using Olive Green Lumiere. I then partially outlined the stencil with a Sharpie. It reminds me of a confessional box, and needs images behind it. I often partially create a spread, and then let it lie dormant until the Muse takes me back to complete it.

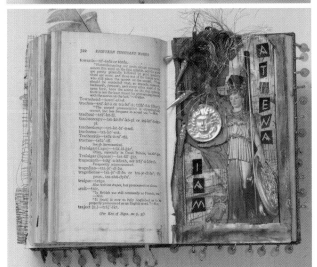

I Am Athena

This tag is from my very first swap. The theme was "I Am" and we were to create something that represented that concept. At the time I had been cast as Athena in a dance performance, so I used the art as an exercise. I was so thrilled with the result that I decided one of the tags should go in my first altered book. I created a "sliding niche" in the back of the book to present and keep the tag in place. I glued 30 pages together. Then I traced around the tag on the pages. I cut out the pages going all the way to the top edge of the page, so the tag could fit into the created niche. In retrospect, I should have glued several pages in front of the niche together, then cut out and created some sort of "bridge", which once glued to the niche area would keep the tag in place.

Antoine de Saint-Exupery said, "He who would travel happily must travel light." Obviously, he had never been to one of Beth Cote's classes. After receiving the supply list for Beth's "Everything but the Kitchen Sink" class, Melissa and I started thinking about the best way to pack.

We decided it would be great to have our basic supplies in a separate container. Each of us had an overnight case from the sixties that had belonged to people who had been instrumental in developing our own love of art.

Through the everyday brainstorming that occurs when two or more friends get together, we decided our overnight cases would be perfect for housing an array of supplies. Decorating them was our way of honoring two special ladies from our past.

These gorgeous make-up cases are truly personal statements to the art muse and a better way to lug around all your art stuff!

Luggage

by Sherry M. Foley and Melissa Jordan

MATERIALS:
Overnight case • Rubber stamps (*Stampington & Co., Postmodern Design, Stampers Anonymous, 100 Proof Press*) • *Tsukineko* Black StazOn ink pad • *Golden* Glazes (Yellow Ochre, Burnt Sienna, Burnt Umber) • *Jacquard* Pearl Blue Lumiere paint • *Plaid* FolkArt Apple Butter Brown Antiquing Medium • *Minwax* Polyurethane Satin Varnish • Collage elements (Tissue paper, decorative papers, copies of family photos, postcards, birth certificates, recipes, letters, deeds, ticket stubs, receipts) • Charms • Game pieces • Manila tags • 1" stiff bristle brush • Masking tape • *USArtQuest* PPA or *Golden* Gel Medium • E-6000 glue

INSTRUCTIONS:
Prep: Apply masking tape to any bands, hinges, closures, or other areas that you want to contrast with decoupaged areas. • Stamp words or images on tissue paper with StazOn ink. Let dry.
Collage: Apply a thin coat of PPA or gel medium to an area of the luggage no larger than four square inches. Begin laying images on top of glue, smoothing from center of image to the edges with your fingers. Continue to adhere collage elements, overlapping images and interspersing with stamped tissue paper until the entire case is covered. • Glue down any loose edges. Let dry completely. • Make design adjustments, if needed, by adding images. You may also lightly sand any rough edges for a more vintage, aged look. Allow to dry.
Glaze: Working from light to dark, begin using the glazes to blend and soften edges where images meet. Allow to dry.
Hardware: Remove tape from masked areas and paint or stain bands and metal pieces. Remember that each piece will be different. The bands on Melissa's piece were antiqued, while mine were painted with Lumiere Pearl Blue to cover the original Williamsburg Blue color.
Finish: Apply several coats of polyurethane varnish, allowing to dry between each coat.
Embellish: Add 3-dimensional elements such as charms, game pieces, bottle caps, etc. using E-6000 glue. Attach a decorated tag, with your name, address, and phone number to the handle.

"Art is neither a profession nor a hobby. Art is a way of being."
~ Frederick Franck

Tips: Since these are vintage, one-of-a-kind items, each will be different. Melissa's overnight case was white, with a very glossy finish. Mine started with really ugly blue leather and a surface that had some tooth to it, making it a bit easier to work with.

You may have to adjust the directions slightly based on the characteristics of your own piece.

Infuse Your Art With Meaning

It's hard to infuse your art with significance, symbolism and emotion. A lot of people don't know where to begin. If this is an important goal to you, be aware that sometimes people will miss your meaning. Don't worry - it is normal and part of the learning process. Here are some suggestions to help you.

1. Go off on a tangent and brainstorm symbols and ideas that surround your themes.
2. Research your idea. Find quotes and poems and bits of stories to fuse your statement.
3. Search out your materials and start to gather stuff. Look for images that reflect your ideas. Do any colors suggest themselves for a palette?
4. Don't forget the power of being ironic. Play with humor as well.
5. Create personal symbolism and use these symbols to write a non-verbal message.
6. Keep your emotion in the front of your mind as you work. If you are working on a piece that you want to be angry, make yourself feel that emotion as you create.
7. Loosen up. Remember art doesn't have to be pretty. Live in the moment as you create.

Take your altered books to the next step by finding or creating a vessel to hold them. Vessels can be wooden boxes, sewn pouches, metal envelopes, or anything you can find that relates to your altered book project. Cigar boxes are good for smaller books. Larger books can have a box made for them or a pouch sewn out of some old fabric scraps. Be inventive: How about an old purse?

Love Letter Box and Necklace

MATERIALS:

Design Originals (Collage Paper #0529 Le Jardin; Transparency Sheets: #0619 Travel, #0622 Beauties) • Wooden book box • 4 wooden feet • Small book • Paris stamp • *Postmodern Design* "secret" stamp • *Clearsnap* Sienna Ancient Page ink pad • *Tsukineko* StazOn ink • *Jacquard* (Lumiere Halo Violet Gold, White Neopaque) • *Golden* (Burnt Umber Light Fluid Acrylic, Glazing Liquid, Gesso) • Armature wire • 33 gauge beading wire • Penmanship transparency sheet • Stacy Dorr, fused glass tags from *Stampington & Co.* • *Nunn Design* (Gold frame DF-2, Violet dd-vl) • *ARTchix Studio* Fabric Art image • Round metal rimmed tag • Old dictionary page • Button • 2 small Gold flower charms • Fibers • Elastic thread • Craft knife or scroll saw • Awl or drill • 1" flat brush • Fine grit sandpaper • *Therm O Web* Zots 3-D • Gel medium • The Ultimate! glue

In this vessel, the altered book is mounted to the outside of the vessel and the inside is used to house love letters. The altered book can be worn as a necklace as well.

Small Book Necklace Box

INSTRUCTIONS:

Niches: Divide the book into two parts. Rub gel medium on the edges of the pages of both sides. Let dry. • Draw a rectangle on both sides and through the cover of the book. • Cut the niches out with a craft knife or drill a hole in the corner of your rectangle and thread a scroll saw through the hole. Note: this needs to be a scroll saw and not a band saw. Carefully saw following the drawn lines. Follow all safety directions that come with the machine. Unthread the blade from the hole and cut the second side and the cover of the book. • Rub gel medium over cut edges. Let dry. • Glue collage material around edges of the hole. • Layer paper and glue transparencies on back of niche. Glue flower charm in the corner.

Outside: Punch a hole with an awl and sew a button closure. Glue elastic thread in between the back cover and the niche. Glue the niche to the back cover as well. • Paint outside of the book with Lumiere and glue collage material over the spine. Adhere transparency over window. Glue Gold frame over the transparency.

Large Book Box

INSTRUCTIONS:

Prep: Lightly sand the entire box. Remove dust with a damp cloth.

Outside: Coat with Gesso. Let dry. • Glue feet on box. • Paint box with Halo Violet Gold and White Neopaque. • Glue Penmanship transparency to the cover of the box. • Take two 12" pieces of armature wire which is very easy to bend and create two small "photo corners" that will hold the book in place on top of your box. Lay your small book down on the cover of the box and fit the photo corners in place. With a pencil, mark 3 places that you will sew over the wire to hold wire in place on each side of the photo corner. • Pierce or drill small holes through the lid of the box. • Sew the photo corners to the lid of the box with 32 gauge wire. • Stamp "secret" on glass tag with StazOn ink. Glue glass tag to circle tag and adhere to the box with The Ultimate!.

Inside: Cut a piece of matboard for the inside wall. The matboard needs to be the width and the depth of your box. • Run a bead of glue along the bottom of the wall and place the wall in the box. Let dry. • Collage the bottom and wall of the box with dictionary pages. This helps to hold wall in place. • Glue a piece of Le Jardin collage paper to the top of box to cover the wire sewing. • Ink or Tea-stain a tag and stamp with Paris Stamp and Sienna Ancient page. Hang fibers from tag. Glue small Gold flower to tag. Use Zots to adhere tag in little section of box. • Glue dice and transparency to inside of box.

"Is this wide world not large enough to fill thee, Nor Nature, nor that deep man's Nature, Art?"
~ Mary E. Coleridge

Have fun making up your own checker and chess pieces. Use your imagination and come up with some wild ideas. Try using the battle aspect to make a statement. Who would you like to see battle: the Old Masters against the Impressionists? The democrats and republicans? The dog lovers and the cat lovers? Here are a couple of ideas.

Chess Set

MATERIALS:
Design Originals Collage Papers (#0600 Dominoes, #0599 Vintage Cards, #0598 Game Cards, #0597 Fortune Cards) • 17" x17" Composite board • Rubber stamps (*Lost Coast Design* Chess Set; *Oxford Impressions* Snap; *Inkadinkado* 5237-P Pocket Watch, 8478 Shoe; *Stampers Anonymous* G208 Hand w/card, P5-821 Chess Pieces; *Paper Inspirations* Moon Face; *Stampendous* C120 Button Cluster; *Renaissance Art Stamp* B9901 small face) • *Memories* ink (Black, Art Print Brown) • *Golden* (Regular Gel Matte; Glaze; Paints: Burnt Sienna, Transparent Red Iron Oxide, Quinacridone Gold, Burnt Umber Light, Asphalt, Ivory Black, Raw Umber, Violet Earth, Burnt Sienna) • *Delta* Instant Age Varnish • Flat brush

INSTRUCTIONS:
Board: Gesso the board. Let dry.
Checkerboard Pattern: Draw out your checkerboard. There are 8 rows of 1$^1/_2$" squares and a 1$^1/_2$" border. • Cut the collage papers into 1$^1/_2$" squares. You will need a total of 32 squares plus a couple extras in case of mistakes. I used parts of four different papers for a varied look. • Adhere the paper squares on the board with gel medium. Roll the square with a brayer to get a good seal. Be sure to skip every other square as you glue to make the checkerboard.
Embellishments: Stamp the border with Memories ink or StazOn. You can stamp inside the blank squares as well with small stamps. Heat set.
Finish: Use a flat brush to paint the empty squares with Quinacridone Gold fluid acrylic. Leave some of the square White. • To get the rich deep color over the entire board, layer these fluid acrylic colors mixed with a little glaze: Burnt Sienna, Transparent Red Iron Oxide, and Burnt Umber Light in that order. Let it dry. Then add more color and wipe it off if needed. This is a slow process. Keep a damp rag beside you. To lighten the color, add more glaze medium. Then to darken the edges and pull in some more color in places, I used the following glazes: Asphalt, Ivory Black, Raw Umber, and Burnt Sienna. Let dry. • Varnish the board with Delta Instant Age Varnish.

Glass Stones Checkers

MATERIALS:
ColorBox (Style Stones-Suits, Chalk Inks: Blue Iris, Dark Brown, Warm Red, Maroon) • *My Sediments Exactly* rubber stamp Y414 • Heat gun
INSTRUCTIONS:
Blue Stones: Ink one side of all 16 stones with the Blue Iris Chalk. Slide the stone onto an opened paper clip and heat set the ink. Let cool. • Ink the other side and the edges of the stone and heat set the ink. Let it cool. • Stamp on one side with the Dark Brown chalk ink and heat set. • **Red Stones:** Follow directions for Blue stones, using Warm Red ink. Top off with Maroon ink. Stamp with the Dark Brown and heat set.

Watch Part Checkers

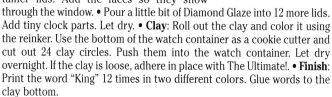

Tip: Be aware that Diamond Glaze will rust and turn metal Blue as it dries. The clay bottoms prevent scratching on your board.
MATERIALS:
Silver Crow (Watch parts, 24 Lids of 3mm watch containers) • 2 bags *Creative Paperclay* Delight modeling compound • Black dye based reinker • *JudiKins* Diamond Glaze • The Ultimate! glue
INSTRUCTIONS:
Prep: Set aside 12 watch faces and 12 groups of clock parts. • **Pieces:** Pour a little bit of Diamond Glaze into 12 watch container lids. Add the faces so they show through the window. • Pour a little bit of Diamond Glaze into 12 more lids. Add tiny clock parts. Let dry. • **Clay:** Roll out the clay and color it using the reinker. Use the bottom of the watch container as a cookie cutter and cut out 24 clay circles. Push them into the watch container. Let dry overnight. If the clay is loose, adhere in place with The Ultimate!. • **Finish:** Print the word "King" 12 times in two different colors. Glue words to the clay bottom.

Tip: A 17" x 17" board has 1$^1/_2$" squares and a border. If you want bigger squares, you will need to design a bigger board. If desired, router the edge of your board for a decorative touch.

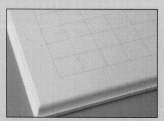

1. Mark off the board.

2. Adhere paper squares with gel medium.

3. Brayer squares to get a good seal.

4. Stamp the borders.

5. Lightly paint the empty squares with Gold.

6. Apply acrylic colors in layers.

7. Add more color and wipe off as needed.

8. To lighten color, add more glaze. Wipe off as needed.

Rusty Nails vs. Buttons

MATERIALS:

Rusty nails • Buttons • 24 *Silver Crow* watch containers 3 mm wide • The Ultimate! glue

INSTRUCTIONS:

Fill 12 watch containers with rusty nails. Fill 12 containers with buttons. • Rub The Ultimate! glue around the edge of the container to seal it closed.

Tip: Buy unfinished wood chess pieces at a craft store or pick up a cheap set at a garage sale.

Tip: Checker pieces need to turn over to be kinged or be able to sit doubled. Here's a set made from Clearsnap Style Stones. One side is stamped for "kinging" and the other side is plain.

Chess Pieces

MATERIALS:

Wood Chess Pieces • *Mayco* (Magic Metallic Rust kit, Dark Bronze Magic Metallic) • *Golden* Black gesso • *Daniel Smith* Venetian Red gesso • Fine grit sandpaper

INSTRUCTIONS:

Lightly sand all pieces. • Separate the pieces into two sides. • Gesso the pieces for one side with Black. Let Dry. Follow with a coat of Dark Bronze Magic Metallic. • Gesso the opposing pieces with Venetian Red. Let Dry. Rust the pieces according to the directions on the Rust kit.

Memory albums celebrate who we were and remind us of how we became who we are. Those of us old enough to remember having "45" records will recognize this book as the storage for all of that old music. Revitalize this relic of the audio past by turning it into an album. This one illustrates school days, but you can theme this project in many different ways. For example, display a collection of old cards and love letters, or give a home to the treasured correspondence between your ancestors. You may even consider turning this book into a file for your collage material or stationary.

School Days Album

MATERIALS:

Design Originals Collage Paper (#0578 Vintage ABC's, #0579 ABC's Dictionary, #0580 School Books, #0591 US Map, #0600 Dominoes) • Record House book • Rubber stamps (*Renaissance Art Stamps* Dragonfly P-9980; *Limited Edition* A-Z stamp JV188D; *Postmodern Design:* Fuzzy Numbers, Fuzzy Alphabet Large, Fuzzy Letters, Run-Skip-Jump Cube, Number Cube; *River City Rubber Works* "I Dream Big" 1903; *Inkadinkado* Bike 8370; *Time to Stamp* Large and Small Spaceship) • *ColorBox* Cats Eye Chalk ink (Warm Red, Yellow Cadmium, Royal Blue) • Alphabet beads • Old game piece • Cardboard poker chip • Thread • Needle • UHU glue stick

INSTRUCTIONS:

Plan: When you design your school album, count the pages and see how many grades you will cover. Don't forget to count kindergarten as one. I decided to let each page reflect a growth in interests by using papers and stamps with different images. For example, the kindergarten page uses "ABC" paper. First grade has games. Second grade has spelling words. Third grade has books. By fourth grade I was interested in travel and geography, so you find bike stamps and map paper. Feel free to theme your pages any way you want.

Pages: Stamp images with chalk inks. Collage papers as desired. • If desired, create a space to hold personal info about that year like the teacher's name and school. Personal information makes the book more meaningful.

Cover: Use a ruler to mark holes evenly around the edge of your album. • Use an awl to poke holes through the cover.

Beading: If you use fibers instead of linen thread, it is easier to use shorter lengths and tie them off, than to try to handle one long length. • Push your needle from the back of the hole toward the front and tie the tail of your fiber to itself to anchor it. • See beading diagram. Blanket stitch through the holes around the album, adding a bead to each stitch. Tie off the end.

Finish: Poke 2 holes in a poker chip. Sew the old game piece to the poker chip. Glue the poker chip to the front cover.

> *"Education is not filling a bucket, but lighting a fire."*
> ~ William B. Yeats

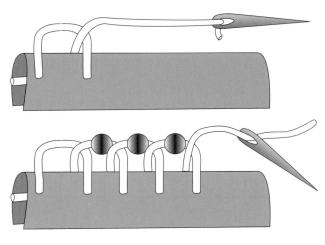

**BLANKET STITCH
BEADING DIAGRAM**

"The most wasted of all days is the one without laughter."
~ e. e. cummings

1. Mark holes for beading.

2. Poke holes through the book cover with an awl.

Altered books and collage create a lot of leftover materials. I don't like to throw anything out, so I put my mind to finding another use for all the leftovers. This binding gives a romantic look to an old book. This book is a loose form. It will wiggle and lay completely flat and open, so it is perfect for journaling.

Exposed Binding Book

MATERIALS:
Design Originals Collage Paper #0594 World Maps • Old book cover • 24" Grosgrain ribbons • 40 pieces of White paper • *7gypsies* Ruler paper • Tag board • Beads that fit on thread and over needle • 3 yards Waxed linen thread • Book binding or tapestry needle • Awl • Old phone book

...continued on page 28

Preparing Signatures

1. Glue Map paper to Ruler paper.

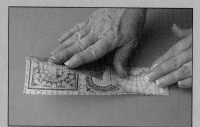

2. Fold in half lengthwise.

3. Place signature into fold of signature cover.

4. Punch holes with awl.

Binding Steps

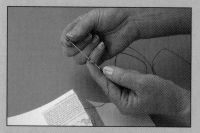

1. Come out hole 2. Add beads.

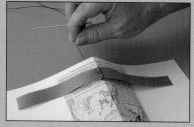

2. Sew down into hole 1.

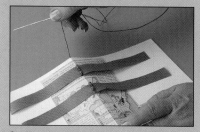

3. For second ribbon, sew out of hole 4. Pick up beads. Sew down into hole 3.

4. Place the ribbon on the third signature between hole 3 and hole 4.

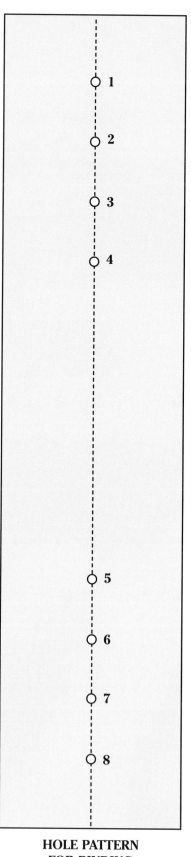

HOLE PATTERN FOR BINDING

1
2
3
4
5
6
7
8

**CLOSE-UP
OF BEADED BINDING**

"Take control of your destiny. Believe in your-self. Ignore those who try to discourage you. Avoid negative sources, people, places, things, and habits."

~ Wanda Carter

continued from pages 26 - 27...

Finish the Cover

1. Glue ribbons to the cover, going across the spine for reinforcement.

"We are what we imagine. Our very existence consists in our imagination of ourselves."

~ Teesha Moore

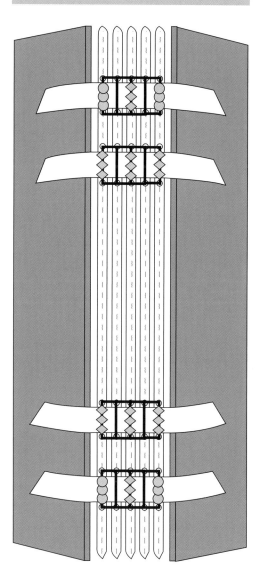

RIBBON PLACEMENT DIAGRAM

Exposed Binding Book

INSTRUCTIONS:

Signatures: Cut 40 pieces of paper 1/4" shorter than the height of the book cover and twice the width minus 1/4". • Fold all 40 pages in half, one at a time. Use a bone folder to get sharp creases. • Nest 8 pages together to make 5 groups of pages. • With a pencil, lightly number each group in the right-hand corner 1-5.

Signature Covers: Cut 5 pieces of ruler paper and 5 pieces of Map paper 2" wide and the length of your folded page. Glue them back to back. Fold in half lengthwise. Place one cover over the outside of each grouping.

Holes: See pattern for hole guide. Fold the hole guide in half lengthwise. Mark the top. Open the first signature to the middle page and lay the guide inside. Place this inside an open telephone book. Punch all holes on the guide through all pages in each signature. The telephone book is like a cradle and will protect your work area from the awl. It will also hold the signature still. Remove guide and set signature aside. Repeat for all signatures.

Binding: Cut 4 ribbons 6" long. • Thread a needle with 36" of waxed linen. • Remember to always sew over the ribbons, not through the ribbons themselves. • **First Signature**: Bring the needle from the inside of the signature out through Hole 2. Leave a 4" tail inside the signature. Add beads. Position ribbon between Holes 1 and 2. See diagram. Push the needle in through Hole 1. Bring needle out Hole 4. Add beads. Place ribbon between Holes 3 and 4. Push needle in through Hole 3. • Bring needle out Hole 6. Add beads. Place ribbon between Holes 5 and 6. Push needle in through Hole 5. Bring needle out through Hole 7. Add beads. Place ribbon between Holes 7 and 8. Push needle in through Hole 8. Push needle out Hole 7 again. • **Second Signature**: Place second signature up against the first. Push needle in through Hole 7 so it is inside the second signature. Bring needle out Hole 8. Position ribbon between Holes 7 and 8. Push needle into Hole 7. Come out Hole 6. Position ribbon between Holes 5 and 6. Push needle in Hole 5. Come out Hole 4. Position ribbon between Holes 3 and 4. Push into Hole 3. Come out Hole 1. Position ribbon between Hole 1 and 2. Push into Hole 2. Come out Hole 1 again. • **Third Signature**: Place the third signature up against signature 2. Push needle into Hole 1. Bring the needle from the inside of the signature out through Hole 2. Add beads. Position ribbon between Holes 1 and 2. Push the needle in through Hole 1. Bring needle out Hole 4. Add beads. Place ribbon between Holes 3 and 4. Push needle in through Hole 3. • Bring needle out Hole 6. Add beads. Place ribbon between Holes 5 and 6. Push needle in through Hole 5. Bring needle out through Hole 7. Add beads. Place ribbon between Holes 7 and 8. Push needle in through Hole 8. Push needle out Hole 7 again. • **Fourth Signature**: Place fourth signature up against the third. Push needle in through Hole 7 so it is inside the fourth signature. Bring needle out Hole 8. Position ribbon between Holes 7 and 8. Push needle into Hole 7. Come out Hole 6. Position ribbon between Holes 5 and 6. Push needle in Hole 5. Come out Hole 4. Position ribbon between Holes 3 and 4. Push into Hole 3. Come out Hole 1. Position ribbon between Hole 1 and 2. Push into Hole 2. Come out Hole 1 again. • **Fifth Signature:** Place fifth signature up against the fourth. Push needle into Hole 1. Bring the needle from the inside of the signature out through Hole 2. Add beads. Position ribbon between Holes 1 and 2. See diagram. Push the needle in through Hole 1. Bring needle out Hole 4. Add beads. Place ribbon between Holes 3 and 4. Push needle in through Hole 3. • Bring needle out Hole 6. Add beads. Place ribbon between Holes 5 and 6. Push needle in through Hole 5. Bring needle out through Hole 7. Add beads. Place ribbon between Holes 7 and 8. Push needle in through Hole 8. Tie tail to inside thread. Knot. • Go back to the first tail in Signature 1 and tie it to the threads. Knot.

Cover: Place the top book cover on the signatures so the ribbons are on top of the cover. Glue ribbons to cover with The Ultimate! • Repeat with back cover.

Lamp and Shade

Tip: Look for an inexpensive lamp. I paid $4.00 for this one at a discount store. The shade is lined with plastic.

MATERIALS:
Design Originals Mounts (#0980 Water Marks, #0990 Round White) • Transparency sheet (#0620 Seaside) • Lamp with shade • *All Night Media* S50K37 Alphabet stamps • *Ranger* Adirondack Color Washes bottle (Denim, Terra Cotta) • Water in Spray Bottle • *Jacquard* Gold/Blue Pearl-Ex ink • *Mayco* (Magic Metallic Steel, Rapid Rust) • *American Tag Co.* hand-held eyelet punch • 1/8" Brass eyelets • Craft knife • *Therm O Web* Super Tape 1/4" roll • The Ultimate! glue

INSTRUCTIONS:
Base: Paint with Magic Metallic Steel. Let dry. • Apply a second coat. Let dry. • Apply a third coat. Spray Rapid Rust while the third coat is wet. Let the rust react. Apply a second spray. If desired, apply a third spray.

Shade: Stamp with Gold/Blue ink. Don't worry if the stamp isn't perfect. • Spray the shade with water. Spray the shade with Denim and Terra Cotta color washes. Spray the shade with more water and more color until you get the look you like. Let dry. • Choose the transparencies and mounts you want on your project. Trace the inside of the mount onto the lampshade. • Use a craft knife to carefully cut just outside the lines. • Tape the transparencies to the shade. Tape the mounts over the transparencies.

Finish: Use a hand-held eyelet punch and setter and set eyelets around the edge of the shade.

The romance of this lamp is more than the rusted base or the dyed shade. When you turn it on, the light shines through the transparencies, lighting these bathing beauties up from inside. Use a low watt bulb in the lamp.

A lamp provides you with illumination. It gives strength and warmth. What do you want to illuminate in your life? Or is there a special place that makes you smile? Take the idea of illumination to the next step and make this lamp represent the light or need for light in your life.

"The ideals that lighted my way, and time after time have given me new courage to face life cheerfully have been Kindness, Beauty and Truth."
~ Albert Einstein

Globe

There is something magical about a globe. It represents not only your world or places you have traveled, but places you have yet to journey to.

MATERIALS:
Metal globe • 2 kinds of napkins • Old dictionary pages • White gesso • *Mayco* Magic Metallic (Bronze, Aqua Blue Patina) • *Golden* (Fluid Acrylics: Burnt Umber Light, Athol Red Medium, Violet Oxide, Quinacridone Magenta, Bright Red Glaze; Glazing Liquid Medium) • *Jacquard* Antique Gold Pearl-Ex • *Krylon* Matte Sealer • *Loew-Cornell* Wash brush • 1" flat paintbrush • #180 fine grit sandpaper • Damp paper towel • Gloss medium

INSTRUCTIONS:
Prep: Lightly sand the globe and stand.
Base: Paint the base with 3 coats of Bronze. • While the third coat is still wet, use a different brush to paint on the Aqua patina. Set aside to let the base react. As the base reacts, add more patina. I dabbed bits on over a period of an afternoon until it had the look I want.
Collage Globe: Gesso the globe. Let dry. • Peel apart the napkins. Their are usually 2-3 ply, be sure to remove all the white backing. Rip the napkins into interesting shapes. • Collage the globe with the napkins and dictionary pages using gloss medium and a 1" flat brush. Lay the napkin down on the globe, and then apply gloss over the napkin itself. • Connect some of the napkins with the dictionary pages to create a bridge between them all. Let dry.
Paint: On a plate, pour some glazing Medium, Athol Red Medium, Violet Oxide and Quinacridone Magenta. With a large wash brush, apply the paint to the globe. Wipe off with a damp paper towel. Continue to add, let dry and wipe a bit off. • Tone the colors together with a last layer of Light Umber glaze. While the glaze is still wet, dip a dry brush into Antique Gold Pearl-Ex and apply it to blank spots on the globe and the globe base. If the glaze dries out, use a bit of glaze medium on the brush. • Seal the paint with Matte Sealer.

Tassel

MATERIALS:
Design Originals Mounts #0988 Small White • *Timeless Touches* Fibers • Tea and walnut stained tags • Collage papers • Rubber stamps (*Postmodern Design* D03-103-G Block of Words; *Paper Inspirations* F0108 Moon face, G1902 Cello; *Stampers Anonymous* P4691 Number Collage, V1-861 Angel; *Limited Edition* JV322-H; *Stampington & Co.* C8244 Eiffel Tower, C8242 Millennium Wheel; *Fred Mullet* 056 Feather; *All Night Media* 550k37 Alphabet Stamp) • *Memories* Chalks A Lot ink pads (Raspberry Cordial, Cinnamon Truffle) • *Jacquard* Pearl Ex (Black, Sepia) • *Ranger* Walnut Stain Distress Ink • *ColorBox* Chalk Inks (Warm Red, Dark Brown) • *Tsukineko* Brilliance Lightening Black ink pad • Assorted beads, charms, coins and ephemera

INSTRUCTIONS:
Mounts/Tags: See directions to Faux Finish mounts and tags. • Stamp with coordinating inks and stamps that reflect the world or journey your globe represents.
Fibers: Cut several fibers 2 feet long. Fold fibers in half and thread them around the North Pole. Pull the ends through and gather both sides so they hang evenly around the North Pole. Take an extra fiber and wind and knot it around all the fibers up close to the pole.
Finish: Tie beads, charms, mounts, tags, compasses, and anything else to the tassel.

Faux Finishes for Mounts

MATERIALS:
Krylon (Black Webbing spray, Chrome, Make it Suede) • *Mayco* Magical Metallic Combos (Steel Metallic, Rapid Rust, Quinacridone Crimson-Copper Metallic-Green Patina, Turquoise Phthalate-Gold Metallic-Aqua Blue Patina, Permanent Violet-Dark Bronze-Aqua Patina, Quinacridone Gold-Brass Metallic-Green Patina)

RUST: Paint mount with Metallic Steel. Let Dry. Do a second coat. Spray Rapid Rust. Do a second coat.
CHROME: Spray mount with Krylon Original Chrome. Let dry.
FAUX SUEDE: Spray mount with Make-it-Suede. Let dry and then spray again with Krylon Black Webbing Spray. Let dry.

Metallic Finishes for Mounts

All metallics are done in 3 coats. First, apply Golden fluid acrylic. Then apply Mayco Metallic Paint. Finish with one of the following patina combinations.
A. Quinacridone Crimson-Copper Metallic-Green Patina
B. Turquoise Phthalate-Gold Metallic-Aqua Blue Patina
C. Permanent Violet-Dark Bronze-Aqua Patina
D. Quinacridone Gold-Brass Metallic-Green Patina

1. Spray mount with Chrome paint for a metallic finish.

1. For faux suede, spray mount with Make-it Suede paint.

2. Then spray with Black Webbing spray.

Faux and Metallic Finishes for Mounts and Tags

Think beyond your ink pads and use spray and faux finishes to make tags and mounts look as varied as a chrome bumper or a rusty tin can.

Mayco Magic Metallics come in a variety of metal paints and patinas. Here are some of our favorite combinations.

Notebooks • Journals • Tags

Everyone needs a notebook and a journal. It's much better than writing the grocery list on scraps of paper. Since you need one anyway, why not make it an artistic expression? This sample is easy to do, inexpensive, and attractive. I hope you enjoy making several for yourself and as gifts for friends.

Altered CD Steno Book
by Lisa Vollrath

MATERIALS:
Design Originals Transparency sheet #0622 Beauties • CD • Blank steno pad • *Hampton Art Stamps* Pocket Watch • *ColorBox* Fluid Chalk Cat's Eye Ink pads (Burnt Sienna, Chestnut Roan) • *Tsukineko* Brilliance Black Pigment Ink pad • Black embossing powder • Old sheet music • Mulberry paper • Assorted fibers • Craft knife • Heat gun • *Xyron* • Glue stick

INSTRUCTIONS:
CD: Tear a strip of sheet music. Glue to CD with glue stick. Trim paper from the center of the CD with a craft knife. • Cut image from transparency sheet. Cut around figure, removing background. Apply to CD using Xyron adhesive. Trim excess transparency from outer edge of CD. • Stamp pocket watch on CD using Black pigment ink. Emboss with Black. • Apply Burnt Sienna and Chestnut Roan inks to CD, tapping lightly around edges. Apply heavily to top section of CD. Gently tap color onto edges of music. Apply heat with heat tool to set ink. • Thread fibers through center of CD.
Cover: Tear a random piece of mulberry paper and glue to cover of book. Glue CD to steno book, over mulberry paper.

Peace Love Joy Tags
by Lisa Vollrath

MATERIALS:
Manila tags • Large paint sample chips • Rubber stamps (*PSX* Antique Alphabet; *Rubber Stampede* Monarch Butterfly; *Melanie Sage* Love Letter) • *Tsukineko* Brilliance Black pigment ink pad • Paper raffia to match paint chips • Hole punch • Heat tool

INSTRUCTIONS:
Position Manila tag on paint chips, avoiding any text. Trace shape onto paint chip. Cut out tags and punch holes with hole punch. • Stamp tags with Love Letter, Monarch and Antique Alphabet. Dry with heat tool. • Cut two short pieces of paper raffia, thread through hole and tie in knot. Unravel raffia if desired.

HELPFUL HINT

Here's a colorful way to recycle old paint chips into lovely tags. If you cut them with a die cut machine, you can make several very quickly.

When you finish your remodel project, make a bunch of these tags with the paint chip colors you used and give them as favors at the housewarming party.

Peace Love Joy Journal
by Lisa Vollrath

MATERIALS:
Design Originals Collage Paper #0547 Dictionary • Blank journal • Rubber stamps (*PSX* Antique Alphabet; *Rubber Stampede* Monarch Butterfly) • *Tsukineko* Brilliance Black Pigment ink pad • Paint sample chips • Frozen juice container lids • Heat tool • E6000 • Glue stick

INSTRUCTIONS:
Lids: Cut 2 1/4" circles from paint samples. Stamp partial butterflies on each sample. Dry with heat tool. • Stamp Peace, Love, Joy in empty spaces on circles. Use heat tool to dry. • Glue to juice lids.
Journal: Cover journal with Dictionary paper. • Arrange lids on journal cover so that butterflies are pointed in various directions. One at a time, align the stamp over the juice lid so the butterfly is pointing in the desired direction. Slide the lid aside, and stamp on the journal cover. Stamp several extra butterflies randomly on journal. When dry, position the juice lids so the butterflies appear to continue from the journal cover inside the lid. Glue in place.

This is a wonderful example of how to fill your art with emotion and meaning. The words and composition work well together to create an expression of gratitude, respect and love.

A Husband Is...

by Carol Wingert

MATERIALS:

12" x 12" canvas • Papers (*7gypsies, K & Co.*) • *Golden* Black gesso • Letters (*7gypsies, K & Co., EK Success, All My Memories, Making Memories, Dymo*) • *Coffee Break Designs* brads • *American Tag Co.* eyelets • *AMACO* Crafting Copper • *Darice* hinges • *7gypsies* (Waxed linen, Walnut ink) • *Liver of Sulphur* • *USArtQuest* PPA

INSTRUCTIONS:

Canvas: Paint edges with Black gesso. Let dry. Adhere large photo with PPA. Add collage papers.

Title: Age copper with Liver of Sulphur. • Cut paper 1" smaller than the copper. Age paper with walnut ink. Create words using various letter styles. "who shares the" is printed on a paper and stitched in place. Adhere to copper with PPA. • Set eyelets. Tie copper to canvas with waxed linen.

Journaling: Computer print journaling. Cut out and insert strips under hinges. Hold together with tiny brads. Adhere to ruler strips. Add pieces of copper trim to the ends of the ruler.

Art expresses the ideal as well as the real. If you have a place you've always wanted to visit, create a canvas using images of the places you would like to see or things you wish to do.

Weekend in Paris
by Carol Wingert

MATERIALS:
12" x 12" canvas • Papers and vellum (*7gypsies, K & Co.*) • *Vintage Charmings* vintage postcards • *River City Rubberworks* stamps • *Ranger* Adirondack ink (stamping, aging) • *Golden* Yellow Ochre glaze • *Jacquard* Brown Neopaque paint • *K & Co.* metal tag • *Magenta.* pewter medallion • *Li'l Davis Designs* key • *Memory Lane* waxed cotton • Postage stamps • Silver clip • Stipple brush • *USArtQuest* (Mica, PPA)

INSTRUCTIONS:
Canvas: Paint canvas edges with Yellow Ochre. Stipple over glaze with Brown paint.
Collage: Adhere papers, postcards, photograph and vellum in place with PPA. Add medallion, key, postage stamps and mica. Tie waxed cotton to "dream" tag. Attach cotton to metal spiral. Adhere to mica with PPA. Stamp words "Paris" "Weekend".

Happy Trails to You! and Happy Memories Too!

Get that "old west" feeling with aged brown papers, a leather-look die-cut and envelope, and the same copper accents you find on a cowboy's "tack". The mesh adds a rough texture to this artfully arranged collage.

The Trail Ride
by Carol Wingert

MATERIALS:
Design Originals Collage Paper #0493 Brown Linen • 12" x 12" canvas • Rubber stamps (*Postmodern Design, PSX*) • *Ranger* Adirondack ink (stamping, aging) • *Clearsnap* Ancient Page ink • *Jacquard* Brown Neopaque paint • *Penny Black* paper • *Magenta* mesh • *Nunn Design* Round Copper Accents • *AMACO* Copper • *7gypsies* (Sticker words, Peace word insert) • *K & Co.* metal tag • *Ellison* Film strip die-cut • Envelope • *USArtQuest* PPA

INSTRUCTIONS:
Canvas: Paint edges with Brown paint. Let dry.
Collage: Age papers with inks. Adhere papers and photograph with PPA. • Add mesh to the right side of canvas. Print the location on paper and adhere to copper. Glue to mesh with PPA. • Add papers, copper accents, and metal tag. • Age the paper for the die-cut and envelope to look like old leather. • Glue envelope in place. Attach small photos to the back of the film strip die-cut. Adhere to page.
Finish: Stamp title and date.

A journal is a very personal art form. It provides a space to express your innermost thoughts. But often, it is far more reaching. My great grandmother passed away before I was born. The only way I have of knowing her is through her journal. It is a part of her I truly treasure. When you are brave enough to record your experiences truthfully, you leave behind a significant bit of history.

Composition Book
by Kathleen Fitzhugh Remitz

MATERIALS:
Mead Composition book • Rubber stamps (*Nina Bagley, Teesha Moore, Limited Edition, Leavenworth Jackson, Acey Deucy, Rubber Baby Buggy Bumpers, Hero Arts*) • *Ranger* Adirondack ink (Espresso, Butterscotch) • Chalk ink pads • Papers (*K & Co., 7gypsies*) • *Nostalgiques* Ruler sticker • Assorted tags • Patina'd Copper Tape • Eyelets • Brads • Old button with shank • 2 Cotter pins • *7gypsies* Nickel bar pin • Child's hair elastic band • *Making Memories* Page pebbles • *Metalliferous* Bezel Copper rings • Assorted hole punches • *JudiKins* stipple brushes • *USArtQuest* PPA

INSTRUCTIONS:
Book: Glue papers to the front and back covers of the book. • Cut a strip of spine paper 3" x height of the book. Glue over spine. Adhere Copper tape to cover the edge of the spine paper.
Closure: Punch a hole in the middle of the edge of the front and back book covers. Set an eyelet in each hole. On the front cover, insert the button shank into the eyelet. Slide a cotter pin through the shank to hold the button in place. • On the back cover, thread the elastic hair band through the eyelet. Hold in place with another cotter pin or tie a knot. • Wrap the elastic around the button to hold the book closed.
Tags: Cut an assortment of tags and decorate them as desired with fibers, brads, eyelets, punches, and collage papers. Tie strings to each tag. Attach string to bar pin. • Glue bar pin to the book cover.
Decorations: Add star brads and page pebbles to the front cover.

"All you need is deep within you waiting to unfold and reveal itself. All you have to do is be still and take time to seek for what is within, and you will surely find it."
~ Eileen Caddy

Collage Letters

MATERIALS:
Design Originals Collage Paper (#0597 Fortune Cards, #0580 School Books, #0595 Vintage Script, #0606 Sea, Sky & Shore) • *Craft Pedlars* Paper mache letters • *Black Ink* handmade paper (P-6250 Gold/Tangerine, TN-2737 Banana Green) • Tissue paper with Purple Diamonds • *Krylon* Gold Webbing Spray • Ransom Letters • Wash paintbrush • *Golden* Gloss Medium

INSTRUCTIONS:

Letters: Apply gloss medium with a wash brush on the letter. Press paper down and apply gloss medium over paper as well. • "A" uses the Fortune Cards, School Books, and Gold/Tangerine papers. "R" uses Vintage Script and assorted collage papers including the tissue paper. "T" uses Sea, Sky & Shore, School Books, and Banana Green papers. • Start with the patterned papers and use strips and organic shapes. Add the solid papers to bridge between the patterns. Let dry.

Decorate: Spray with Webbing. • Spell the words "Aspire" on the "A", "Realize" on the "R", and "Transform" on the T with Ransom letters.

Words are powerful. Create a personal shrine to the word that encourages your creative process. The first step is to choose the word that inspires you. I chose "Art". Then choose other words that also describe your creative process, beginning with the letters in the word you chose. For example: **A**spire, **R**ealize, **T**ransform.

Go beyond your creative process. All art does not have to be beautiful. Is there some hurt, or some word that has haunted you in your life? Spell it out and use the first letters in that hurtful word to transform that word into something affirming.

Put a new twist on tags and make some tag folders that are just large enough to make a great card.

Tag Booklet

MATERIALS:
3 square 5$\frac{1}{2}$" tags • 1 tag 4$\frac{3}{4}$" x 5" • 2 tags 2$\frac{1}{2}$" x 4$\frac{3}{4}$" • Assorted stamps • *Memories* Art Print Brown ink pad • *ColorBox* Chalk ink pads • *Jacquard* Lumiere Paints (Bronze, Gold, Purple) • *Krylon* Gold Metallic Webbing spray • *Black Ink* Moriyama Paper • Fibers • Silk ribbons • *Artistic Wire* wire • Beads • *Uchida* punches (Asian, 2" circle) • *Fiskars* border punch • $\frac{1}{4}$" *Therm O Web* Super Tape • Glue

INSTRUCTIONS:
Folder: Paint 3 large tags with Lumiere. Let dry. • Rip off the upper two thirds of one of the large tags for the inside pocket. Tape pocket to the back tag around the edges. • Spray both sides of the folder with Gold webbing. Let dry.

Spine: Cut a piece of Moriyama Paper for the outer spine 1$\frac{1}{4}$" x 6$\frac{1}{2}$". • Put glue on the wrong side of the Moriyama paper. This will be the outer spine of the folder. Lay the two tags centered on the Moriyama paper with a bit of room between the two. • Cut another piece of Moriyama paper $\frac{1}{2}$" x 5$\frac{1}{4}$" for the inner spine. Glue this paper to the inside of the spine. Fold the flaps of the outer spine to the inside of the folder.

Celebrate

INSTRUCTIONS:
Folder: Sponge with Chalk inks. Collage and stamp all sides as desired. Punch the square border along the outer edge. Add wire and beads to the tag hole on the front and weave wire through punched holes.
Tag: Sponge with Chalk inks. Stamp and collage as desired. Tie tags and charms with ribbons.

Dragonfly

INSTRUCTIONS:
Folder: Stamp Dragonfly on Mulberry Paper. Glue to Cover. • Punch Asian symbol on front cover. • Decorate inside of folder with quote. • Thread fibers through the tag hole in the front cover. Thread beads and charms onto fibers. **Tag**: Punch a 2" hole in both tags so the holes line up. Sandwich mesh between tags to cover the hole. Glue tags together. Paint tags with Lumiere. • Stamp, color and decorate as desired. • Wire tags together through the tag hole and add beads as desired. Put tags into pocket.

Decorated Matchboxes

by Lisa Vollrath

Small cardboard matchboxes can be recycled into beautiful works of art with the techniques in these two projects.

FOR DREAM NECKLACE

MATERIALS:

Small matchbox • Blue acrylic paint • White artist's pastel • *Daler-Rowney* Silver Pearl Pearlescent Liquid Acrylic • Iridescent glitter glue • Fine point markers • Chalks • *Dymo* Labelmaker • Blue mulberry paper • Blue cardstock • Star-shaped confetti sequins • *DMC* Gold metallic embroidery floss • Gold braid • Flat gold bead • Polyester fiberfil • *Creative Paperclay* Delight Air Dry Modeling Compound • *AMACO* (Moon Push Mold) • Large needle • Paintbrush • Hole punch • *Weldbond* glue • Glue stick

FOR SHINE PIN

MATERIALS:

Small matchbox • *Daler-Rowney* Mazuma Pearlescent Liquid Acrylic • Yellow acrylic paint • Yellow artist's pastel • *Dymo* Labelmaker • *DMC* Gold mulberry paper • Ochre cardstock • Star-shaped confetti sequins • Gold metallic embroidery floss • Flat gold bead • Polyester fiberfil • *Creative Paperclay* Delight Air Dry Modeling Compound • *AMACO* Sun Push Mold • Gold glitter glue • Fine point markers • Chalks • Large needle • Paintbrush • Pin back • *Weldbond* glue • Glue stick

FOR DREAM NECKLACE AND SHINE PIN

INSTRUCTIONS:

Outside: Cut 2" strip from mulberry paper. Coat matchbox with glue stick and wrap with mulberry paper. If printing shows through paper, coat with glue and wrap again. • Tear off excess paper. • Cut 3/8" strip from cardstock. Load into labelmaker and write words. Tear ends of label. Glue to top of matchbox. • Apply glitter glue to lower section of matchbox. While still wet, apply large star sequin to corner of box. Let dry completely.

Cords: Pierce one end of matchbox tray twice with large needle to create holes for pull. • If creating necklace, punch two holes in other end with hole punch to create holes for hanger.

Inside: Paint tray with acrylic. Let dry. • Cast face using mold and Delight Modeling Compound. Let face dry completely before painting. • Paint face with Liquid Acrylic. Let dry. • Add details to face with fine point markers. Add color to cheeks with chalks. • Glue a small amount of fiberfil into tray. Apply liberal amount of Weldbond to back of face and glue into tray. Glue several small star-shaped sequins into tray around face.

Finish: Thread large needle with floss. Create pull by threading floss through bead, into one hole in tray, back out second hole, and through bead again. Tie a knot below the bead, and trim floss to desired length. • If creating necklace, thread braid through holes in tray. Trim to desired length and knot to create hanger.

Matchboxes

1. Wrap box with paper.

2. Tear away excess paper.

3. Print label with a Dymo label tool.

4. Apply Gold glitter glue.

5. Punch holes for the pull.

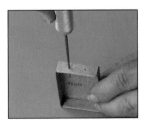

6. Paint the inside of box.

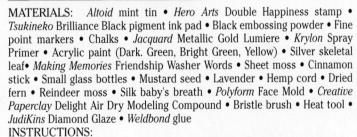

Tiny Shrine

by Lisa Vollrath

Decorate a candy or mint tin to store small objects or amulets. As an option turn the tin into a small shrine. Either way, you will enjoy the experience.

1. Basecoat tin with primer.

2. Paint the exterior.

3. Sponge exterior. Let dry.

4. Coat tin with Diamond Glaze.

MATERIALS: *Altoid* mint tin • *Hero Arts* Double Happiness stamp • *Tsukineko* Brilliance Black pigment ink pad • Black embossing powder • Fine point markers • Chalks • *Jacquard* Metallic Gold Lumiere • *Krylon* Spray Primer • Acrylic paint (Dark. Green, Bright Green, Yellow) • Silver skeletal leaf• *Making Memories* Friendship Washer Words • Sheet moss • Cinnamon stick • Small glass bottles • Mustard seed • Lavender • Hemp cord • Dried fern • Reindeer moss • Silk baby's breath • *Polyform* Face Mold • *Creative Paperclay* Delight Air Dry Modeling Compound • Bristle brush • Heat tool • *JudiKins* Diamond Glaze • *Weldbond* glue

INSTRUCTIONS:

Paint: Base coat tin with spray primer. Let dry. • Paint exterior of tin with Dark Green acrylic. Paint interior with Bright Green. Let dry. • Sponge exterior of tin with Bright Green and Yellow acrylic. Let dry. • **Outside**: Coat tin with Diamond Glaze. While wet, apply skeletal leaf to tin and coat with Diamond Glaze. Let dry. • Stamp double happiness on tin with Black ink. Apply Black embossing powder. Heat. • Glue happiness word washer to corner with Weldbond. • **Inside**: Cast face using face mold and Delight Modeling Compound. Let dry completely before painting. • Paint face with Metallic Gold. Let dry. • Add details to face with fine point markers. Add color to cheeks with chalks. • Apply Diamond Glaze to inside front lid. While wet, position fern in lid and coat with Diamond Glaze. Let dry. • Glue sheet moss into tin with Weldbond, leaving space for face. Glue face in place and surround with reindeer moss and silk baby's breath blossoms. • Fill bottles with mustard seed and lavender. Tie small pieces of hemp cord around bottles below stoppers. • Glue cinnamon stick and bottles in place with Weldbond. Let dry completely before handling.

Peace Tin Necklace

by Lisa Vollrath

MATERIALS:

Go Lightly mint tin • *Hero Arts* Chinese Peace stamp • *Tsukineko* Brilliance Black pigment ink pad • Black embossing powder • *Jacquard* Sunset Gold Lumiere • *Krylon* Spray Primer • Red acrylic paint • Chinese text paper • Hemp cord • Flat gold bead • Sea sponge • Heat tool • Drill and small drill bit • Bristle brush • *JudiKins* Diamond Glaze • E6000

INSTRUCTIONS:

Prep: Drill holes on either side of tin below cap. • Basecoat tin with spray primer. Let dry. • Paint tin with Red acrylic. Let dry.

Collage: Tear Chinese text paper into a small irregular shape. • Coat tin with Diamond Glaze. Apply text paper to one side of tin. Coat paper with Diamond Glaze. Let dry. Lightly apply Sunset Gold Lumiere to tin with sea sponge. Let dry. • Stamp Chinese Peace on front of tin with Black pigment ink. Apply embossing powder. Heat. • Glue flat bead to bottom of tin.

Cord: Cut 3 pieces of hemp cord, fold in half and insert into hole in bead, gluing in place. Thread hemp cord through holes in tin. Cut to desired length and knot to create hanger.

1. Drill holes below cap.

2. Paint with Red.

3. Apply Diamond Glaze. Add paper. Coat paper with Glaze.

4. Sponge with Sunset Gold.

BASIC MATERIALS

Bristle brush • Tape • E6000 • Glue stick • Photos

FOR MY DOG WEEVIL BOOK

MATERIALS: *Design Originals* (Collage Paper #0584 Puppies at Play, Printed Mounts #0987 Vintage Books) • *H.E. Harris & Co.* Silver Dollars coin holder • Cardstock (Red, Natural) • Rubber Stamps (*PSX* Antique Alphabet; *Anita's* Ornamental Alphabet; *Rubber Stampede* Paw; *Hampton Art Stamps* Little Classic Heart) • *Memories* Dye ink pad (Red, Black) • Acrylic paint (Royal Blue, White, Red) • *Krylon* Krystal Clear spray sealer • White artist's pastel • *Forster* Woodsies squares • *Li'l Davis* (Red Wood Circle Letters, Wood Tile Letters) • Vintage milk bottle cap • Small dog biscuit • Red button • Red rayon floss • *Renaissance Art* Art Keepers Glass Dome • Red ticket • Star-shaped brad

FOR ALYSSA BOOK

MATERIALS: *Design Originals* (Collage Paper #0585 Little Girls, Mount #0990 Round White) • *H.E. Harris & Co.* Silver Dollars coin holder • *Anita's* Ornamental Alphabet stamps • *Tsukineko* Versamark ink pad • Silver embossing powder • *My Type* Silver Stencil Letters • *Daler-Rowney* Silver Pearl Pearlescent Liquid Acrylic • Acrylic paint (Fuchsia, White) • Cardstock (Pink, Natural) • *Making Memories* (Simply Stated Expressions, Emotions Charmed Words, Wisdom Charmed Phrases, Children Charmed Quotes, Friendship Washer Words, Round Alphabet Charms, Metal Frame) • *Renaissance Art* Art Keepers Glass Dome • Pink button • Silver heart-shaped button • Bottle cap • Star-shaped sequin • Tiny Pink rhinestone • Dried daisy • Round metal-edge tag • Pink *DMC* Pearl Cotton • Pink ticket • Pink fibers • Fuchsia silk ribbon • Heat gun • Mallet

INSTRUCTIONS

Book: Remove third page from coin holder to create a 2 page book. Base coat inside with colored acrylic. Let dry. Dry brush with White acrylic. Let dry.

Photos: Cut photos into 1 1/2" circles or tape photos to small mounts. Arrange photos in coin slots.

Outside covers: Cover exterior of holder with patterned paper.

EMBELLISHMENTS

FOR MY DOG WEEVIL BOOK:

Cut 1 1/2" circles from Natural and Red cardstock, and from large Woodsie. Drag Woodsie circle across Red dye ink pad to stain. Stamp with paw using Black dye ink. Glue in place. • Stamp Red heart on Natural cardstock. Glue in place. • Cover heart with Glass Dome, gluing around outer edge with E6000 to anchor. • Glue Red cardstock circle in place. Glue star-shaped brad onto circle. • Stamp initial with Ornamental Alphabet using Red dye ink. Glue in place. • Stamp "My Dog Weevil" on small square Woodsies. Glue in place. • Glue "ARF" letters, milk cap and ticket in place. • Tie rayon floss through holes in button and glue in place. • Paint dog biscuit Red with acrylic. Let dry. Glue in place.

FOR ALYSSA BOOK:

Cut 2 Pink and 3 Natural 1 1/2" circles. • Glue Pink circles into niches. Glue an alphabet charm and heart-shaped button on top. • Glue Natural circles into niches. Tie pearl cotton through holes in Pink button. Glue a button and a dried daisy on the Natural circles. Apply word "Love" from Simply Stated Expressions to the third Natural circle, and cover with a Glass Dome. • Glue Little Girls paper to a round tag. Apply words from Simply Stated Expressions to tag. Tie with silk ribbon and glue over niche. • Flatten bottle cap with mallet. Glue star-shaped sequin to center of flattened cap. Glue into niche. • Glue Washer Word to edge of photo. Fill center with tiny rhinestone. • Glue Charmed Quote over niche. Glue Charmed Phrase and Charmed Word to edges of photos. • Tear ticket in half and glue in place. Adhere Stencil Letters to bottom of holder with E6000. • Apply Simply Stated Expressions as desired. • Tie fibers around spine of book.

Here's a great idea for a fun, small altered project. Turn coin holders into a photo and memorabilia portfolio. This project becomes the perfect pet lover's book or tribute to a family member.

Coin Holder Books

by Lisa Vollrath

Double Foliette

by Audrey Freedman

MATERIALS: *Stamp Oasis* (Double Foliette, Rubber stamps, Gold Luna Lights ink) • *Tsukineko* Black StazOn ink • *Ranger* ink (Butterscotch, Terra Cotta, Espresso) • *ColorBox* Amber Fluid Chalk ink pad • *Stampendous* White shrink plastic • White bond paper • *K & Co.* metal frame • Scrap leather • Sponge • *Sailor* glue pen • *Pacer* Zap-A-Gap glue • Tacky glue

INSTRUCTIONS: **Inside**: Paint the inside with Gold Luna Lights ink. Let dry. • Stamp "Find your Path" in Black StazOn on White paper. Tear around words. Stain with Butterscotch ink. Rub Terra Cotta pad around the edges. Adhere inside the front cover with glue pen. • Stamp "Celestial Dreams images with Black StazOn on glass slides. Let dry. Dot one of the slides with Magenta, Gold, and Copper Luna Lights. Gently put slides together and slide away from each other. Let dry. Glue in place with Tacky glue. • **Outside**: Rub a plain White paper with Butterscotch ink. Stamp a Diamond border with Terra Cotta ink in rows. Stamp "Small Triskel" in Espresso ink randomly. Trim the paper to fit the front and back of the foliette. • Rub Amber chalk on the shrink plastic and wipe off. Stamp the "Celestial Dreams" face image in Black StazOn. Shrink according to manufacturer's directions. Trim plastic as needed to fit into the frame. Glue to the frame with Zap-A-Gap. • **Binding**: Trim a leather scrap to fit as a book binding. Sponge Black StazOn around the edges. Adhere with Zap-A-Gap. • **Finish**: Glue frame to front cover with Zap-A-Gap.

Mother Earth Foliette

by Audrey Freedman

MATERIALS: *Stamp Oasis* (Single Foliette, Rubber stamps, Gold Luna Lights ink) • *Tsukineko* Black StazOn ink • *Ranger* ink (Butterscotch, Pink, Terra Cotta, Espresso) • *ColorBox* Fluid Chalk ink pad (Amber, Purple) • *Stampendous* White shrink plastic • Copper wire • Sponge • *Sailor* glue pen • *Pacer* Zap-A-Gap glue • Tacky glue

INSTRUCTIONS: **Prep**: Paint the entire Foliette, inside and outside, with Gold Luna Lights ink. Let dry. • **Inside**: Stamp the inside cover with a solar image in Terra Cotta. Stamp text with Black StazOn. • Stamp the "Winged Goddess" image with Black StazOn on a glass slide. Let dry. • Dot one of the slides with Magenta, Gold, and Copper Luna Lights. Gently put slides together and slide away from each other. Let dry. Glue in place with Tacky glue. • **Outside**: Stamp a feather with Butterscotch ink. Let dry. • Rub Amber chalk on the shrink plastic and wipe off. Stamp the "Mother Earth" image in Black StazOn. Edge the plastic with Purple ink. • Shrink according to manufacturer's directions. • Wrap plastic with wire. Glue to the cover with Zap-A-Gap.

Glass Slide Covers

Turn a microscope slide mailer into a heartfelt keepsake or an inspiring piece of art. The samples below will spark your imagination and light your creative spirit.

The Key to My Heart
by Lisa Vollrath

MATERIALS:
Design Originals Collage Paper #0500 TeaDye Keys • Microscope slide mailer • Rubber stamps (*PSX* Antique Alphabet , *Hampton Art* Little Classic Heart) • *Jacquard* Super Copper Lumiere • *ColorBox* Fluid Chalk ink pad (Burnt Sienna, Chestnut Roan) • *Tsukineko* Brilliance Black pigment ink • Small Manila tag • Dried flower • Burgundy silk ribbon • Skeleton key • Craft knife • *Weldbond* glue • Glue stick

INSTRUCTIONS:
Tag: Age the edges of the tag with Burnt Sienna ink. Stamp "I Give To You" in Black pigment ink. Let dry. • Tie a silk ribbon bow through the hole in the tag.
Inside: Place the key in cut-out section of slide mailer. • If the key is too bulky to allow the mailer to close, trace around the key with a craft knife. Remove key and gently cut along the line, cutting through a few layers of board, but not all the way through to back side of the mailer. Use a knife blade to gently remove the cut area, creating a deeper niche for the key. • Basecoat the interior and edges of slide mailer with Copper Lumiere. Let dry. • Stamp "The Key to My Heart" and heart inside the mailer using Black pigment ink. Let dry. • Tie a silk ribbon to the key. Glue the key into niche.
Cover: Cover the front and back of the mailer with Keys paper. Age the edges with the Burnt Sienna ink pad. • Adhere tag to the front of the mailer. Gently glue dried flower to the bottom front of the mailer, overlapping the tag.

Asian Foliette
by Audrey Freedman

MATERIALS:
Stamp Oasis (Single Foliette, Asian Vintography, Rubber stamps) • *Tsukineko* Black StazOn ink • *ColorBox* ink pads (Warm Red Fluid Chalk, Gold pigment) • Black acrylic paint • *Stampendous* White shrink plastic • Black permanent marker • *Aitoh Papers* (Yuzen, Asian tissue)• *Sakura* Crystal Lacquer • Sponge • *Pacer* Zap-A-Gap glue • Tacky glue • Glue stick

INSTRUCTIONS:
Front cover: Cut a small piece of printed Yuzen paper 1/2" x 2". Cut Asian tissue 1" x 2. Glue to the front of the foliette. • On White shrink plastic, stamp "Geisha" in Black StazOn. Trim and shrink. Adhere to front with Zap-A-Gap. • **Inside**: Stamp "Kanji Characters" randomly over the inside of the foliette in Gold. • Select an Asian girl from "Asian Vintography" and gently sponge with Warm Red ink. Lay glass slide over artwork and trim. Secure to glass with Crystal Lacquer. Adhere slide in foliette with Tacky glue. • Stamp "Honor the Seasons" on shrink plastic and trim, leaving some border. Draw around the edge with Black permanent pen. Shrink. Adhere inside foliette with Zap-A-Gap.

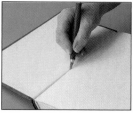

Prepare the Book Cover for a Portfolio or a Clutch Purse

Prepare the book cover for new use. Remove the pages, reinforce the spine, add a button closure.

1. Cut the text block pages out of the book.

2. Reinforce the spine with duct tape, overlapping a portion of the front cover.

3. Add more tape, overlapping the back cover.

4. Punch holes through the back cover to tie ribbon for a button closure.

5. Sew a large button to the cover.

Book Clutch Purse

Once in a while, I use pages from a book in my collage work and all that I have left is the cover. So, here are some ideas for all those left-over covers!

MATERIALS:
Old book • Matboard • Assorted seed and facet beads • Beading thread • Beading needle • *me & my Big ideas* woven label "Live laugh love" • Lining fabric • Button • Needle • Thread • Awl • Craft knife • Hot glue gun • *Therm O Web* (1/4" Super Tape, Super Tape sheets, HeatnBond Hem Tape) • Duct tape

INSTRUCTIONS: **Prep:** Remove the text block from the book cover, cutting carefully between the end pages and the cover. • Cut a piece of duct tape and line the inside of the book spine. Overlap the duct tape on each cover to reinforce the spine.

Closure: Punch 2 holes with an awl on the edge of the front cover. Sew a button to the book board.

Lining Side Flaps: Stand the book on a sheet of paper. Trace around the triangle. Add 1/2" seam allowance. • Cut four side flaps from lining fabric. • With right sides facing, pin two flaps together. Repeat for the other pair.
• Sew flaps together. Turn the triangles right side out. Slip stitch the ends shut and press flat. • Hot glue the flaps to the spine of the book.

Purse Lining: Measure length of the purse. Add 1/2". Measure width of the purse. Add 1/2". • Cut one piece of lining to this size, press the edges under to fit the size of the purse. • Press a hem along the edges of the lining with hem tape. Add 1/4" Super Tape to the inside edges of the lining.

Portfolio

The old world look of this journal adds a sophisticated twist to a portfolio. From vintage buttons to old ribbon, this portfolio says a lot about you.

MATERIALS:
Book • Lining fabric • 2 large buttons • Ribbon • Waxed linen thread • Duct tape • Needle • Awl • *Therm O Web* (Super Tape roll & sheets, HeatnBond Hem Tape)

INSTRUCTIONS:
Prep: Remove the book text block from the book cover. Carefully cut between the end pages (the first and last page in a book) and the covers.

Spine: Measure the book spine. Cut a piece of duct tape to size and line the inside of the book spine with the duct tape. Be sure to do this on the inside where the lining will cover up the tape. Be sure to overlap the duct tape onto the book board as well a bit. This will reinforce the spine.

Closure: Decide where you want the button closures and punch two holes with an awl on each cover. • Tie a ribbon to the shank of the button that will be on the back cover. Sew your buttons to the book boards, one on each side. • To hold book closed, wrap the ribbon from the back around the button in the front.

Inside: Measure the length and width of the book cover and add 1" to all sides. Cut one piece of lining to this size. Press the edges under to fit. • Use hemming tape to hem the edges of the lining. • Apply Super Tape around the hem of the lining. Adhere the full sheets of Super Tape to the center of the lining fabric. Remove the backing from the full sheets. Press the lining to the book. Remove the backing from the tape on the edges. Place and press the edges of the lining to your portfolio.

Assembly: Apply Super Tape sheet to the center of the book covers. See diagram. Position lining. Remove backing from Super Tape in the center of the book covers NOT along the hem. Smooth the lining fabric over the exposed sheet of Super Tape. Fold the lining away from the book edges. • Hot glue the edges of the flaps to the sides of the book covers. See diagram. • Remove the backing from the Super Tape on the lining edges. Smooth lining over flaps. • Measure the bottom of your purse. Cut a piece of mat board to this size. Check the fit by pushing it down into the bottom of your purse. Cover with lining fabric. Place inside purse bottom.

Beading: Thread a beading needle with enough beading thread to match twice the length of the book plus 6". Knot the end. Hide the knot in the lining. Bring the needle out at one corner. String beads. Push the needle through fabric lining at the opposite corner. Whip stitch the beaded strand to the edge of purse lining. Do this to the other side.

Closure: String beads on elastic thread and create a loop to go over the button. Sew to lining.

Finish: Make a beaded tassel. Hang tassel around the button. • Glue a label or decoration to the front of purse.

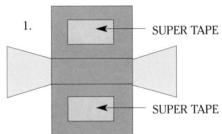

1.   SUPER TAPE

    SUPER TAPE

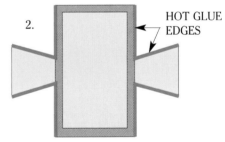

2.   HOT GLUE EDGES

1. Trace the edges of book to make a pattern for side flaps.

2. Cut 4 side flaps from lining fabric.

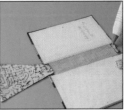

3. Hot glue flaps to the spine.

4. Press a hem in the purse lining with hem tape.

5. Smooth lining onto the book cover.

6. Hot glue flaps to the book edges.

7. Remove tape backing from the edges of lining.

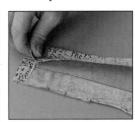

8. Cover matboard with lining fabric.

Beth Cote

Beth is a well-known professional artist who works with mixed media and book arts.

Her main focus is Altered Books. Beth travels across the country teaching popular paper arts workshops at retreats, shops and conventions.

Beth's teaching schedule and altered book ideas are on her Web site at

www.alteredbook.com

SUPPLIERS - Most craft and variety stores carry an excellent assortment of supplies. If you need something special, ask your local store to contact the following companies:

Design Originals, 817-877-0067, Ft. Worth, TX
7gypsies, 800-588-6707, Mesa, AZ
All Night Media, 800-842-4197, Norcross, GA
AMACO, 800-374-1600, Indianapolis, IN
ARTchix Studio, 250-370-9985, Victoria, Canada
Artistic Wire, 630-530-7567, Elmhurst, IL
Clearsnap, 800-448-4862, Anacortes, WA
Crafter's Pick 510-526-7616, Albany, CA
Darice, 800-453-1527, Grant's Pass, OR
Delta, 800-423-4135, Whittier, CA
EK Success, 800-524-1349, Clifton, NJ
Foofala, 402-330-3208, Omaha, NE
Golden, 800-959-6543, New Berlin, NY
Hero Arts, 800-822-4376, Emeryville, CA
Inkadinkado, 800-888-4652, Woburn, MA
Jacquard, 800-442-0455, Healdsburg, CA
JudiKins 310-515-1115, Gardena, CA
Krylon, 800-457-9566, Cleveland, OH
Li'l Davis Designs, 949-838-0344, Irvine, CA
Limited Edition, 650-594-4242, San Carlos, CA
Lost Coast Design, 408-244-2777, San Jose, CA
Magenta, 450-922-5253, Quebec, Canada
Making Memories, 801-294-0430, Centerville, UT
Mayco, 800-781-2529, Albuquerque, NM
me & my Big ideas, 949-589-4607, Rcho Santa Margarita, CA
Nunn Designs, 360-379-3557, Port Townsend, WA
Papers by Catherine, 713-723-3334, Houston, TX
Plaid, 800-842-4197, Norcross, GA
Postmodern Design, 405-321-3176, Norman, OK
PSX, 800-782-6748, Santa Rosa, CA
Ranger, 800-244-2211, Tinton Falls, NJ
Renaissance Art Stamps, 860-567-2785, Burlington, CT
River City Rubberworks, 877-735-2276, Wichita, KS
Rubber Stampede, 800-632-8386, Whittier, CA
Saunders, 800-341-4674, Readfield, ME
Silver Crow, 412-521-4938, Pittsburgh, PA
Stamp Oasis, 702-878-6474, Las Vegas, NV
Stampendous, 800-869-0474, Anaheim, CA
Stampers Anonymous, 440-250-9112, West Lake, OH
Stampington, 877-782-6737, Laguna Hills, CA
Saunders, 800-341-4674, Readfield, ME
Tara Materials, 770-963-5256, Lawrenceville, GA
Tsukineko, 800-769-6633, Redmond, WA
USArtQuest, 517-522-6225, Grass Lake, MI
U.S.Games Systems, 800-544-2637, Stamford, CT
Zettiology, 253-638-6466, Renton, WA

MANY THANKS to my friends for their cheerful help and wonderful ideas!
Kathy McMillan • Jennifer Laughlin
Patty Williams • Marti Wyble
Janie Ray • Donna Kinsey
David & Donna Thomason

Tote Bag from a Book Cover

I like to use large books. 11" x 15" work very well for this project. Books with colorful covers are preferred.

1. Cover matboard with lining fabric.
2. Hem the lining with iron-on hem tape.
3. Apply Super Tape around the edges of the inside of the lining.

4. Hot glue the tube to the bottom of the book covers.
5. Smooth lining over center Super Tape.
6. Fold back edges of the lining. Hot glue tube to the side of book.

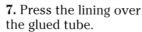
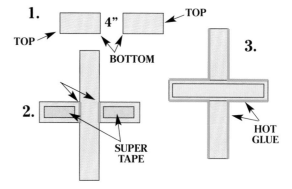

7. Press the lining over the glued tube.

MATERIALS:
Old book • Book handles • Lining fabric • *Dritz* Large Grommets • Matboard • Duct tape • *Nunn Design* Book Corners • Waxed Linen • Awl • *Therm O Web* (1/4" Super Tape, Super Tape Sheets, HeatnBond Hem)

INSTRUCTIONS:
Prep: Remove the book text block from the book cover. Carefully cut between the end page (the first and last page in a book) and the cover. Cut the book boards off of spine if you are using a book that still has a spine.
Matboard: Measure the width of your book. Cut a piece of mat board to the size of the width and 4" wide. Cover matboard with lining material.
Lining: Line up the front cover, covered matboard and the back cover. Measure this and add 1" inch to the length and width. Cut lining to this size and press the edges under 1/2" using hem tape. • Apply Super Tape around the hem on the inside of the lining.
Tote sides: Measure two lengths and a width of your book. Calculate the sum. Then add 3". This will be the length of your fabric. The width is 9". Cut one. • Fold the fabric in half to 41/2" x length. Sew a 1/4" seam along the long edge. Turn the tube inside out.
Assembly: Place the book covers face down so the bottoms are lined up 4" apart. (See diagram.) Line up the center of the tube with the center of the book. Hot glue the edges of the tube to the bottom of the book covers. • Apply Super Tape sheet to the center of the book covers. See diagram to position lining. Remove backing from Super Tape in the center of the book covers NOT along the hem. Smooth the lining fabric over the tape. Fold the lining away from the book edges. • Hot glue the edges of the tube to the sides of the book covers. See diagram. • Remove the backing from the Super Tape on the lining edges. Smooth lining over tube fabric.
Handles: Mark holes for handles. Punch holes with the awl. Set grommets. Tie handles to tote with waxed linen.